A LEADER WITH COURAGE:
THE IMPACT OF CONGRESSWOMAN CARDISS COLLINS

A LEADER WITH COURAGE:
THE IMPACT OF CONGRESSWOMAN CARDISS COLLINS

Jasmin N. Dobson, M.Ed.
&
Frank E. Dobson, Jr, Ph.D.

MILL CITY PRESS

Mill City Press, Inc.
2301 Lucien Way #415
Maitland, FL 32751
407.339.4217
www.millcitypress.net

Library of Congress Control Number:

Paperback ISBN-13: 978-1-66288-285-2

Hard Cover ISBN-13: 978-1-66288-286-9
Ebook ISBN-13: 978-1-66288-287-6

TABLE OF CONTENTS

CHAPTER 1
CARDISS HAS HUMBLE BEGINNINGS

C ardiss Collins was born on September 24, 1931, to Finley, a laborer, and Rosia Mae Robertson, a nurse. Her parents, the Robertsons, were industrious people who instilled in her the values of hard work, dedication, and a concern for others. Although Cardiss was born in St. Louis, Missouri, her parents moved their family to Detroit, Michigan, when she was ten years old. She grew up in Detroit, where she graduated from the Detroit High School of Commerce. Upon graduation from high school, she moved to Chicago to live with her maternal grandmother, Emma Robertson. There, she attended night classes at Northwestern University, earning a business certificate in 1966 and a degree in professional accounting in 1967. After that, she worked for the State of Illinois in an office.

She was a young Black girl who was determined to succeed, showing a strong work ethic and commitment. When talking about her childhood, she once said the following: "When I was growing up, I was told that I had to work harder and do better because I was a little Black girl." The parents of Cardiss instilled in her an ethic to work, earn an education, and succeed.

Young Cardiss with her parents

CHAPTER 2

THE LOVE STORY OF GEORGE COLLINS AND CARDISS COLLINS

As a young woman, Cardiss met George Washington Collins, and they married in 1958. They had one child, a son, Kevin Collins, who was born in 1959. From 1964 to 1970, her husband served as a member of the Chicago City Council. In 1970, George W. Collins was elected to Congress, serving until 1972. He was devoted to helping the people in his Congressional district in Chicago have better lives for themselves and their families.

Cardiss always helped her husband with his political career. She once said, "I'd like to say that I ran all of his campaigns." Her husband, a Democrat, was a strong advocate for the people of their district in Chicago. He served a district with a majority being Black, hard-working families, and he also represented people of other diverse backgrounds. His mission was to serve the people of Chicago, and Cardiss shared that same goal.

Due to an airplane accident near Midway Airport, George died on December 8, 1972. On that date, he was returning to Chicago to organize and purchase toys for an annual Christmas party for the children and families in his district. After his death, he was mourned by many people. The Chairman of the Congressional Black Caucus at the time, Congressman Louis Stokes, said this: "The legacy which George Collins leaves is an abiding devotion to the people." George Collins, a congressman and public servant who served in the United States Army during World War II with the Army Corps of Engineers, was an American hero.

Cardiss, George, and Kevin Collins

CHAPTER 3

Cardiss Shows Courage Through Tragedy

L ike her late husband, Cardiss Collins was dedicated to helping people. She showed commitment to their shared dreams and goals for the people of Chicago. She had been incredibly involved in her husband's service to their district and community. The people in their district wanted her to replace her husband because they believed that she was determined to represent them and their families as she served in Congress.

Cardiss showed great courage when she agreed to run in the election to fill her husband's vacant seat in Congress, the Seventh Congressional District. At first, she was reluctant to run for her late husband's seat in Congress. She was a quiet person and not outspoken. She was someone who preferred to work behind the scenes. She said, "I never gave politics a thought for myself. When people started proposing my candidacy right after the crash, I was in too much of a daze to think seriously about running." Not only did the people in their Black district want her to run, but so did Mayor Richard J. Daley. Most importantly, their son, Kevin, then just thirteen, also wished for her to continue her husband's legacy. Kevin told his mother, "I want you to take his place, to keep the Collins name going." She ran to continue the legacy of her husband and their family, the work of helping others and serving the public good.

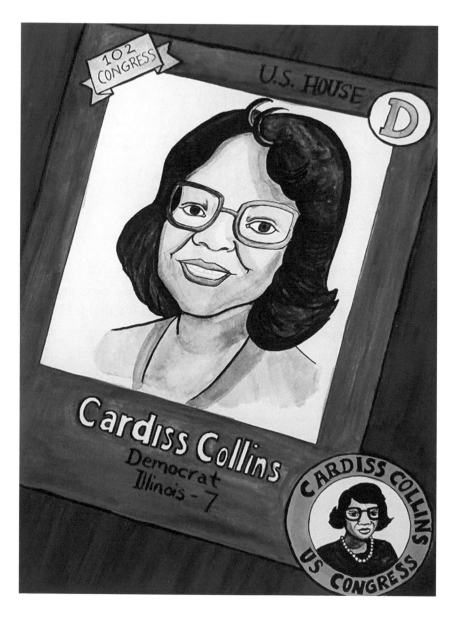

Cardiss Collins Runs for Congress

CHAPTER 4

CARDISS WINS

When Cardiss Collins ran to fill the vacancy of her late husband, she won, receiving 92 percent of the vote. On the date of June 5, 1973, she became the first Black woman to represent the State of Illinois in Congress! She was the first Black woman from a state in the Midwest to serve in Congress. She was also the fourth Black woman to serve in Congress.

Shirley Chisholm of New York was the first Black woman elected to the US House of Representatives in 1969, serving from 1969 to 1983. Yvonne Brathwaite Burke of California was the second Black woman to serve in Congress, from 1973 to 1979. Barbara Jordan of Texas was the third Black woman to serve in Congress, from 1973 to 1979.

Cardiss truly made history, joining the ranks of such illustrious women in politics. This modest young woman, whose mother had told her when she was a girl that she had to "be better and work harder," had done just that. Cardiss Collins, through her election, showed that even a little Black girl from a humble background can, with determination and courage, one day become a United States Congresswoman.

Women Who Made History!

CHAPTER 5
CARDISS GOES RIGHT TO WORK

When you are appointed or elected to a new job, it is important that you get to work quickly. You want to show people that you can do the job. Cardiss Collins did just that! Even though she was shy, Cardiss found her voice! She became a strong spokesperson for those who had no voice. In 1973, her first year in office, she said that her goal was "to provide better living and working conditions for people (from the Chicago neighborhoods that she represented) and other low- and moderate-income people throughout the country." During her many years in Congress, Cardiss would spend eight days each month back in Chicago and her district to listen to the concerns of the people she represented. She cared about them, and she listened intently and closely to their words and ideas.

Cardiss was a strong advocate for people, and she cared about their health and safety. For example, in 1991, she helped sponsor a bill to bring stricter controls on the transportation of toxic materials. Cardiss fought for a clean environment, which is a critical issue because we all want to be able to have clean air to breathe and clean water to drink. This issue is especially important today, and so her work effort to have more controls on toxic waste is a current one. As a politician, through hard work and commitment, she reached impressive milestones, including becoming the first African American and first woman selected as a Democratic Whip At-Large. During her first term in Congress, she also served on the Committee on Government Operations. With each new accomplishment, Cardiss continued to show concern for others. She knew that she was representing the people of her district and setting a standard for women and ethnic minorities who might follow in her footsteps. Between 1983 and 1990, Cardiss Collins was the only Black woman serving in the House of Representatives. She was a true spokesperson and advocate, holding her own as a voice for women, minorities, and the poor.

Cardiss Collins: A Voice for the Public Good

The Impact of Cardiss Collins:

"Cardiss Collins was a champion of women and African Americans everywhere, whose work was productive in areas of American life and is still being felt in our country."

Congresswoman Eleanor Holmes Norton
February 8, 2013

"Statement from Congresswoman Eleanor Holmes Norton (D-DC) on the Passing of Former Congresswoman Cardiss Collins of Illinois." Targeted News Service (USA), sec. U.S. Congress, 8 Feb. 2013. NewsBank: America's News Magazines, https://infoweb.newsbank.com/apps/news/openurl?ctx_ver=z39.88-

CHAPTER 6

CARDISS LEADS AND SERVES

As a Congresswoman, Cardiss Collins also served on an important group of Black elected officials, the Congressional Black Caucus (CBC). From 1979 to 1981, she served as the second woman to serve as Chair of the Congressional Black Caucus. She also later served as Vice Chair of the Congressional Black Caucus. The Congressional Black Caucus was founded on March 30, 1971, by thirteen founding members, including her late husband, George Collins. It exists to help the cause of Black Americans and others.

To date, this is the list of all the Black women who have served as Chair of the CBC, with their term as Chair of the CBC in parentheses:

- The first was Yvonne Braithwaite Burke of California (1976-1977)

- The second was Cardiss Collins of Illinois (1979-1981)

- The third was Maxine Waters of California (1997-1999)

- The fourth was Eddie Bernice Johnson of Texas (2001-2003)

- The fifth was Carolyn Cheeks Kilpatrick of Michigan (2007-2009)

- The sixth was Barbara Lee of California (2009-2011)

- The seventh was Marcia L. Fudge of Ohio (2013-2015)

- The eighth was Karen Bass of California (2019-2021)

- The ninth was Joyce Beatty of Ohio (2021-2023)

Like Cardiss Collins, these women were leaders who made history. When Cardiss was asked to define the word "leadership," she said this: "leadership is seeing something that needs to be done, and just going and doing it." Cardiss Collins was a fitting example of leading by "doing" something," serving others through dedication and determination. She got things done.

The Congressional Black Caucus

The Impact of Cardiss Collins:

"She left a mark. The mark was the raising of urban
issues in a significant way."

Congressman Danny K. Davis
February 2013

CHAPTER 7
CARDISS ADVOCATES FOR WOMEN, MINORITIES, AND ALL

During her time as Chair of the Congressional Black Caucus (CBC), Cardiss Collins pushed hard for Congress to make Martin Luther King, Jr's. birthday a federal holiday. She even criticized President Jimmy Carter for his record on civil rights and his failure to gather sufficient support for the passage of the King Holiday. The birthday of Dr. King became a national holiday in 1983, and all of America now celebrates this holiday. However, the fight to make the birthday of Dr. King a national holiday began in 1968, with a bill introduced by Representative John Conyers of Michigan and other congressmen. It took fifteen years for the birthday of Dr. King to become a national holiday, one where the entire nation has a day off from school and work to reflect on the life of Dr. King and the legacy of the Civil Rights Movement. The Dr. Martin Luther King, Jr. National Holiday was signed into law in 1983, by President Ronald Reagan. Cardiss Collins fought during the entire effort to establish Dr. King's birthday as a holiday for all Americans. In 1979, when Cardiss served as Chair of the CBC, she said, "The contributions to the nation of Dr. King can't be measured in dollars. He caused the greatest peaceful social revolution since the founding of the country." Cardiss was one of the leading politicians to fight for the King National Holiday, which is now a day when all Americans reflect on the values of social justice and service to others.

Cardiss Collins spoke out on issues that she felt were important to improving the lives of others. As a Black woman who fought for her community and poor people, she also said, "We will no longer wait for political power to be shared with us, we will take it." She was unafraid to speak "truth to power." She fought for the rights of people, through her sponsorship of important bills. She sponsored the Universal Health Care Act and the Healthy Security Act, which were aimed at addressing health disparities. She was an advocate for airlines safety, and she authored bills requiring warning labels on dangerous toys. She also promoted bills that addressed health issues for women.

Cardiss Collins introduced the Equality in Athletic Disclosure Act on February 17, 1993. This was a bill to make things better for women athletes at colleges and universities. She was inducted into the Women's Sports Hall of Fame in 1994 because she was such a strong ally for women in sports. She wanted to help make sports equal for girls and women. She was also an enthusiastic fan of sports, as she once asked the entire United States House of Representatives to join her "in congratulating one of the greatest teams in the annals of basketball and one of the greatest players ever, Michael Jordan." She said this in 1996, following the Bulls winning their fourth NBA title that year. This is an example of how Cardiss Collins was a true citizen of Chicago and a sports fan!

Cardiss at her desk in Congress

The Impact of Cardiss Collins:

> "A pioneer of her time, she was an effective policy-maker and representative, where she set the bench-mark for many members of Congress to emulate."
>
> Former Congressman Bobby Rush
> February 2013

McCANN Associated Press, HERBERT G. "Former Congresswoman Cardiss Collins dead at 81." Associated Press: US Politics & Government Online, sec. Domestic, 7 Feb. 2013. NewsBank: America's News Magazines.

CHAPTER 8
CARDISS IS A ROLE MODEL FOR TOUGH TIMES

The story of Cardiss Collins is about a person who faced a setback, the unexpected death of a loved one. Her story exhibits strength and love through a painful personal experience. As a Congresswoman, she spoke with conviction, even though she was not a naturally outspoken person. She said, "I was basically an introvert, but once people learned I had something to say, I gained confidence. But it took a long time to come out of my shell and realize I was here, doing this alone." Here, she is speaking of having to be away from her son for weeks at a time because her job as a Congresswoman required her to be in Washington, DC, while her son was being cared for by her mother, in Chicago. Congresswoman Collins would see her son, Kevin, on weekends during her trips back to Chicago to speak and meet with those she represented in Congress. She was a devoted mom who loved her son.

She also maintained a powerful sense of duty to the people of Chicago, as she wanted to "provide better living and working conditions" for them. Her list of accomplishments in Congress is numerous. She was a strong advocate for Black businesses, and she also took on the airline industry, advocating for more equitable hiring practices and more opportunities for Black and other minority-owned businesses in the aviation industry. She did all this while being a single parent, raising her son long-distance. She showed incredible commitment and courage. She planted seeds of character and accomplishment for young people and those who have followed her.

Cardiss Serves Others

CHAPTER 9

CARDISS DID HER JOB AND WAS RECOGNIZED

Cardiss Collins fulfilled her job as a Congressperson at a remarkably important level for a long time, for almost twenty-four years. Perhaps because of her quiet nature, Cardiss Collins was overlooked, which sometimes happens. But the record shows that she did her job well, and for that she is a role model. Sometimes, you will do an excellent job and not get the recognition you deserve. This may be the case because you do not seek attention or popularity. Cardiss did not seek fame or attention. Her goal was to help others and to do a good job. As she said, see "something that needs to be done, and just going and do it." "Do it" is a great legacy for anyone!

Cardiss Collins had an outstanding career in Congress, standing up and speaking up for Black people, women, minorities, and all Americans. She decided to retire from politics in 1997. She returned to Chicago and later moved to Alexandria, Virginia. Once retired, she spent more time with her family, sang in her church choir, and did volunteer work in the community.

Cardiss Collins passed away on February 3, 2013, in Alexandria, Virginia. She left one son, Kevin, and a granddaughter, Candice. She was a fun-loving Black woman, mother, and leader who was loved and admired. The New York Times's headline about her passing reads: "Cardiss Collins, Fighter for Equality and the Poor, Dies at 81."

Indeed, Cardiss made a lasting impact. She was elected to the Black Women's Hall of Fame in 1982. She was a member of two churches: Friendship Baptist Church of Chicago, Illinois, and the Alfred Street Baptist Church of Alexandria, Virginia. She was also a member of the National Association for the Advancement of Colored People (NAACP), the Chicago Urban League, the Links, the Coalition of 100 Black Women, and the National Council of Negro Women. Cardiss also received honorary degrees from several colleges and universities, including Spelman College, Barber-Scotia College, and Winston-Salem State University.

She was also a proud member of Alpha Kappa Alpha Sorority, Inc. There is a United States Post Office named in her honor: Cardiss Collins Post Office, 433 Harrison St. Chicago, IL. There is also a high school named in honor of her husband, George W. Collins: The Collins Academy High School, 1313 Sacramento Dr., Chicago.

A Post Office Named in Honor of Cardiss

The Impact of Cardiss Collins:

"Wow, what a true pioneer, who really needs to be recognized. She should have been recognized so much earlier for her accomplishments."

Former Chicago Alderman, Deborah Graham
February 2013

https://www.oakpark.com/2013/02/12/trailblazer-cardiss-collins-81/

CHAPTER 10

A LEGACY LESSON FOR ALL AND QUESTIONS TO PONDER

There are numerous interviews and videos of Congresswoman Cardiss Collins on C-SPAN and other platforms. She left a legacy that lives on.

Take time to learn more about this incredible leader. Her story deserves to be known. The narrative of how she continued the legacy of her husband, George W. Collins, is a love story to be admired and cherished. The speeches Cardiss Collins made, the bills she sponsored, and the time she took an unpopular position, but stood for justice and fairness, these are the reasons that she is a role model to be admired.

In an interview with the Visionary Project, Congresswoman Collins says, "I would advise young African Americans to learn our history." She also says, "It is our responsibility to tell our stories to our families." Her story is one that should be shared with young people and families.

We ask you to read the following questions and apply them to your life.

1. Why do you think Cardiss continued her husband's work after the airplane accident? Have you ever helped someone complete a goal or job?

2. Cardiss was a pioneer and the fourth Black woman to serve in Congress. She was also the second woman to serve as Chair of the Congressional Black Caucus. Have you ever had a time when you did something new or were the first one to take the initiative?

3. Cardiss served in Congress for almost twenty-four years, helping others. Have you ever served others, whether in your school or community?

4. Cardiss was a member of Alpha Kappa Alpha Sorority, Inc., an organization of women who serve others. Are you involved in groups that help others?

5. Think of a time when you showed courage in the face of a difficult situation.

6. Finally, we ask that you think about how you will remember and share the impact of Cardiss Collins, who was truly "a leader with courage."

Cardiss Leaves a Legacy

Printed in the USA
CPSIA information can be obtained
at www.ICGtesting.com
LVHW071938011123
762649LV00017B/656